WHO'S IN YOUR
ORBIT?®

Beyond Facebook –
Creating Relationships That Matter

Mike Muhney & Max J. Pucher

Published by Carpenter's Son Publishing, Franklin, Tennessee

Dilbert comic licensed from the Dilbert Store, Order #1759512

Cover Design: Debbie Manning Sheppard

Interior Layout Design: Suzanne Lawing

Printed in the USA by Worzalla Publishing

978-0-9830415-0-4

"The most important part of the human mind is its ability to imagine."

- Albert Einstein

TABLE OF CONTENTS

Who Are All These "Friends," Anyway?
From "Friends" to "Frienditutes"
Bringing Relationships into Balance
Orbits of Resource and Influence
Where We're Headed

Why Strong Relationships Matter
The Chinese Principle of Guanxi
Politics Built on Personal Relationships
The Importance of "Social Capital"
Happiness is Contagious
Friends With Real Benefits

What Makes Relationships Strong — and Orbital
The Four Components of Relationship Strength
Time: Being Present and Attentive
Intensity: The Emotional Connection
Trust: Earned Over
Reciprocity: A Mutual Choice
Positively Strong: The Orbital Bond

ACKNOWLEDGEMENTS

From Mike:

As is usually the case, it's impossible to thank everyone who has been a part of my life's Orbits. To those I may have overlooked: please forgive me, but know that you've helped develop my appreciation of personal relationships and the views that have led me to become a relationship-oriented software entrepreneur. ACT!™ and VIPorbit® are tributes to your contributions and advice. I would, however, like to especially thank both Kristi Elmendorf and Bas Reichgelt who not only go back with me to the ACT!™ era but who also are the brain trust with me again at VIPorbit®.

I do, however, wish to specifically acknowledge my parents, Richard and Priscilla Muhney, who had the enormous challenge of helping to guide me on life's path in an honorable fashion. Memories of my mouth being washed out with a bar of soap continue to guide me to honesty today. If I never told you before, Dad, please allow me now to say thanks. And Mom, you are my life's best example of focusing on and caring for others before oneself. I am incapable of fully reaching the standard that you represent, but I will always strive to do so. I have tried to do my best with my kids, Michael, Katy, Derek, and Orion, along with my grandkids, Justice, Nia, Sophia, Dylan, Ella, Kylie, and Abbie.

I would also like to give special thanks to IBM for hiring me in 1975 as a recent university graduate and putting me in its inimitable and intense sales school. Despite its title, its most important lessons were not about how to sell, but about how to deal with people in the business world — how to regard them, and what to know about each and every one of them. To my teachers and mentors at IBM: you will never know how much of the design of ACT!™ and VIPorbit® you helped to provide. I am grateful for my many years with you, and for your nurturing of my career in ways that could not help but spill over into my personal life.

I also wish to express my deep appreciation for Max, the co-author of this book and my partner in business. I have enjoyed our far-ranging discussions, and I greatly respect your perspective on the many aspects of life we have explored. You have become a very dear friend, and that overshadows any and all business interests that we share. I am proud to know you and to be counted by you as a friend.

Lastly, I am grateful to my wife Janet for her boundless love and her saintly patience in providing that love to me every day. I know that I have my flaws, yet your love is unconditional. You are truly a priceless gift to me.

From Max:

As much as Mike and I share, we are quite different, so I won't try to list all the people I could acknowledge as important in my life. There would simply be too many, and once I started, I would be terribly worried about accidentally leaving someone off the list. Plus, where would I stop? There have been a number of people who were very relevant to the direction of my life without even being aware of their influence or having any intention of helping me. I will limit myself to mentioning only those who have been most essential for this book:

I am grateful to my parents, who didn't try to turn me into someone other than I was. My mother was an anesthesiologist and was always there for me with advice when I needed it. With five children, she didn't have much time, but she taught me the value of quality in relationships. She died at nearly 90 years of age, just a few months after she stopped driving her car. My father was a teacher and a fun person, though not one for deep exchanges with his children. He didn't try to imprint me with his perspective on life, for which I am still grateful for. When he died, he took the mystery with him.

My son Bernard confirmed to me that true art is a unique expression that needs neither justification nor accolades. He started to compose electronic music at age 16, and a few years ago he received a master's degree in cinematography from the London Film School. He always wanted to share his work, but when I criticized, he wouldn't even think about changing a thing.

Finally, I need to thank Mike for starting two adventures with me: an exciting new business, and the journey of writing this book together. We share an intuitive trust in each other that is hard to find. I am honored to be his friend and proud that he trusts me to be his partner.

To everyone else who has been a part of my life, thanks for putting up with my ways!

PREFACE

We live in an age of hyper-connectedness. Surrounded by vast, technology-enabled social networks, we're more connected than ever before. We're connected via Facebook friendships, LinkedIn connections, Twitter feeds, Google+ Circles, and no doubt even newer types of links by the time you read this.

But how many of these relationships actually mean anything? And, viewed together, are they simply a loosely linked social network, or are they something more powerful and sustaining? Are they, in fact, Orbits?

In this book, we present a pathway to stronger relationships and orbital networks. We discuss what makes relationships strong, how to counteract the relationship-weakening pressures of today's social-media culture, and how to turn your networks into Orbits: spheres of resource and influence that support you in a meaningful way.

What we discuss in this book isn't rocket science. While it applies some insights from the science of social networking, most of it is good, old-fashioned common sense. Science can teach us a lot on a human level, but it takes common sense to make the most of these teachings and use them to understand and strengthen your relationships.

"But if it's common sense," you may ask, "why do I need a book to explain it to me?" The simple answer is this: when it comes to relationships, common sense is not common at all.

The understanding developed in this book has required a lot of accumulated experience from a wide range of people. At one end of the range are those who create relationships the way most of us breathe — unconsciously, and generally without too much effort. At the other end are those who struggle to get over the very basic human hurdles that interactions with others can represent.

Wherever you may find yourself in this range, you can benefit from a better understanding of how your connections with others influence you — and of how you can interact with them to build strong relationships. Whether you're focused on business, family, or friendships, applying the insights in this book will make your relationships and social networks stronger, unlocking a vast potential of mutual opportunity. You can grasp this opportunity to create deeply sustaining, collaborative Orbits.

But don't just take our word for it. Keep an open mind and make your way through the chapters. With a little bit of effort, some practice, and a determination to succeed, you'll soon be on your way into Orbits.

With regards,

Mike and Max

 **CHAPTER ONE**

Who Are All These "Friends," Anyway?

What does the word "friend" mean to you? How about "relationship"?

Chances are, as you've incorporated social media into your daily life, your definitions of these words have changed dramatically in recent years. Getting in touch with others has never been easier. You're connecting with more people than ever before — and sharing information with them all simultaneously.

Being able to reach others so easily is a great advance. But how deep are most of these connections, really?

We ourselves come from a time when real friends could be counted in the low double digits — so it was easy to maintain a mental "database," not just of memorized phone numbers, but also of substantive personal information connecting us to each friend. Today, technology connects us all with a dizzying number of friends and professional contacts in a new and highly public way, but something has been lost. Our friendships have increased dramatically in quantity, but they've diminished in quality.

Let's take a closer look at what's contributing to the loss of substance in all these relationships — and at how we can recapture the personal value that makes them meaningful.

From "Friends" to "Frienditutes"

Scott Adams, creator of the comic strip *Dilbert*, ran a series of cartoons focusing on the shallowness of Facebook relationships. In it, he used the term "Frienditute" for a certain type of not-so-genuine Facebook friend.

Licensed from the Dilbert Store, Order #1759512

While most of us "friend" people on Facebook with more sociable motives than those portrayed in *Dilbert*, Adams' point that social-media friendship has become a less-satisfactory substitute for real friendship is well taken.

At first glance, the reason these friendships are less than satisfying seems pretty obvious: we simply can't spend as much time on each relationship when we have hundreds of them instead of a few dozen. Less time per relationship means lower-quality relationships, right? Well, that's part of the problem, but let's look a little deeper.

First, let's look at how the typical social-media relationship is initiated: You get an email invitation from someone on a service such as Facebook or LinkedIn, saying something like, "So-and-so would like to connect with you." Oh, and by the way, this "friend doesn't even take the time to write a truly (hell, even *untruly*) personal note, but just sends the default invite. So, offered the options to accept or decline, you decide to accept. Perhaps you even make the extra effort to respond with a personal note (unless you too have been lulled into the complacency of the default relationship path).

Once you've accepted this connection — allowing this person access to all sorts of personal information on your page — you never hear from him or her again. You have a "friendship" initiated with essentially zero personal contact. You can observe each other's publicly shared details and status changes without responding at all, if you want. We like to call this *relational voyeurism*.

Now you have an impersonally initiated relationship in which each of you shares information with each other—but it's the same information you share with lots of your other "friends." Sure, you're demonstrating a certain amount of trust in sharing details of your life with these folks, and trust is an important quality of a strong relationship, but now the trust is impersonal. Instead of creating deep bonds by trusting specific people with information that you share only with them, you are trusting *everyone* with much of your information (perhaps dangerously, if you're not careful) — and deepening bonds with no one. Just ask the writer for *Slate* magazine who posted three fake birthdays on Facebook in a single month and had 16 people send birthday greetings all three times — without appearing to notice the repetition.

While on some level most of us sense the lack of value in these relationships, the temptation to add more and more of them is hard to resist. Having lots of Facebook friends, LinkedIn connections, or Twitter followers seems valuable because it validates your popularity in a clearly measurable way ("Whoa, I have twice as many friends as that person!") Numeric measures like these create both pressure and allure — which may explain the unnerving trend in some emerging software products to provide numbers ranking people's social value.

Somehow, we've all taken a wrong turn. In the process of trying to fulfill the potential of the new relationship options that expand our reach so amazingly, we've altered the way we think about relationships. We've accepted the idea of friendship without personal contact or effort. We've bought into the quantification of popularity and personal value. We've adjusted our notions of privacy and trust in a way that makes them less meaningful — and less available to strengthen our bonds with others. And, by altering our thinking this way, we've turned away from the true potential within our relationships: the prospect of a unique, personal connection that is truly valuable to both parties.

Fortunately, that potential is still there. And we don't have to turn our backs on technology to find it. We simply need to seek a more balanced mindset — and the tools to go with it.

Bringing Relationships into Balance

Social-media tools are great for some aspects of connecting with people, but not so good for others, as the following table shows:

Social-media tools are great for...	But they're not so good for...
• Establishing contact with a large number of people	• Deepening individual relationships
• Minimizing the effort needed to create friendships	• Maximizing the value of each friendship for both parties

• Publicizing information and requests that you want lots of people to see	• Fostering trust with others through privately shared information
• Mobilizing people for large events or social actions	• Motivating people to support each other one-on-one, in significant ways
• Empowering change and innovation in business through a broad, non-hierarchical sharing of knowledge	• Nurturing nascent business deals and R&D efforts before they're ready to be revealed publicly
• Quantifying and analyzing numerically measurable aspects of relationships (number of friends, frequency of page visits)	• Cultivating the "heart" and "soul" of a relationship

So, what's out of balance here? Despite the many positive—and, indeed, *revolutionary*—aspects of social media listed on the left side of the preceding table (which we'll discuss in more detail later in this chapter), there's also a "Me-centric" theme that recurs in several places: "Look how many friends I have!" (or connections, or followers); "Here's lots of info about *me*!"

As this book was going to press, Facebook was in the processing of unveiling its new "Timeline" layout, a glossy-looking design for each user's personal page that makes that person's entire Facebook history gorgeously and readily available, like an advertisement for his or her life. As a thrilled reviewer on gizmodo.com gushed, "It feels like a monument to yourself, and to how incredibly far you've come... If the notion of the digitized self pleases you,

Facebook is your best new altar." Well, great, but allowing others to worship at your public altar isn't likely to create meaningful relationships with them.

What's lacking in today's social media (unless you truly do care only about yourself) is the "Them" perspective: the awareness that true relationships are reciprocal. You need to show interest in other people, not just expect them to be interested in you. You need to make an effort to get to know them—who they really are, not just their public personas — and find the unique ways that you connect with them. Only through a personal, two-way connection — and respect toward each other's privately shared information — can you build the foundation of trust essential for a close and mutually beneficial relationship.

Countering the prevailing "Me" perspective with a "Them" perspective requires an adjustment in thinking. Because the usual metaphor for connections among a group of people — the social network — doesn't embody the sense of depth and reciprocity implicit in a "Them" perspective, we'd like to suggest a more evocative metaphor for the groups of deep, dynamically interacting relationships at the heart of your social network: *Orbits*.

Orbits of Resource and Influence

Dictionary.com includes the following among its definitions of the word "orbit":

• *the usual course of one's life or range of one's activities*

• *the sphere of power or influence, as of a nation or person*

When you're truly connected to the other people in your life, you influence them and they influence you. Like the gravitational forces that cause orbiting planets to rotate around a common point, emotional connections pull you into orbital relationships with others around common goals.

We use the term "Orbits" to describe the groups of people who are connected to you, not just by happenstance, but by strong reciprocal bonds and common goals. The people within your Orbits take on roles that balance and resonate with yours in a stable way, fostering productive and powerful interactions.

Orbits don't exist apart from social networks, but within them. The term "social network" can describe any interconnected structure of individuals linked by specific types of interdependency (such as kinship, friendship, common interests or beliefs, or shared knowledge or prestige). While we tend to think of social networks as a technological phenomenon, enabled by social media, they've actually been around as long as humans have associated in groups. The concept of a social network goes back at least as far as the work of the German sociologist Georg Simmel in the early 1900s, who studied and wrote about the forms of interaction that associate individuals into larger groups.

Your social network includes the whole enormous range of people associated with you — friends, family, colleagues, acquaintances, and so on.

Your Orbits, on the other hand, are more like the inner cores of your social circles. For example, if you picture your social network as a set of circles such as those in Google+ ("Friends," "Family," and so on), your Orbits would be like smaller, circular subsets within each circle, containing only those people with whom you share strong, two-way connections — connections based on something deeper than just public interactions.

We like to think of these Orbits as your "spheres of resource and influence" tweaking the Dictionary.com definition slightly to emphasize the tremendous resources your Orbits provide. They make up the subset of your social network in which you invest particular time and effort to maintain strong connections. They consist of relationships that you nurture, and that support you in return.

Since they are built from two-way relationships, your Orbits are not "Me-centric." And because personal trust is essential in these relationships, your Orbits require private, personal interactions to sustain their bonds — the type of interactions becoming increasingly rare in a world.

Where We're Headed

We believe the irrationally exuberant "Me-centric" mindset that dominates social media today is a bit like the dot com bubble and the housing boom in our not-so-distant past: it's heading for a reality check. The illusion that there is no cost to our neglect of privacy-based, reciprocal relationships (as we embrace the rapid expansion of our public friendship networks) is just that — an illusion. As more and more people are burned by the consequences of oversharing — and as the cost in loss of true friendship becomes apparent — the need for a more balanced mindset will emerge.

Social networking technology has provided an unprecedented capability to enhance the breadth of our business and personal connections, with many positive consequences. By connecting a wide range of people previously isolated from each other — not just geographically, but also socially, across diverse layers of society and business hierarchies — today's social-networking technologies have fostered revolutionary changes at a previously unheard-of pace.

The "Arab Spring" of 2011, in which Twitter and other social media communications played an important role in enabling democratic uprisings in such countries as Tunisia and Egypt, is one noteworthy example of the power of these technologies. In business, a good example is Apple's AppStore, a socially-networked infrastructure bringing together application developers and customers for fast-paced, collaborative development of an incredible array of innovative iPhone and iPad apps — more than Apple could possibly have dreamed up by keeping all development in-house.

These examples show the dramatic benefits that social-networking technology can provide with respect to public sharing of information and ideas, acting as a driving force for innovation (a topic on which Max has written extensively in his blog, which can be found at http://isismjpucher.wordpress.com/).

However, in our rush to embrace this technology and the broad public benefits it provides, we need to be sure we're not leaving something vital behind: the human aspect of our close connections with others.

What's needed now is a way to take that dazzling new breadth and add depth, so that you're not only connecting to more people, but connecting to many of them more deeply and effectively as well — revealing galaxies of Orbits all around you.

 **CHAPTER TWO**

Why Strong Relationships Matter

When you're reeling from a lost business deal or the break-up of a personal relationship, do you post your deep feelings about it on Facebook? Do you tweet about it? Or do you call someone close to you for some one-on-one support?

Likewise, imagine yourself at a moment when you're bursting to share some great news. You can post your news online and get a burst of brief "congratulations!" comments from friends who caught it passing by in their message streams. But will that response be as satisfying as an in-person smile or hug from someone who takes the time to celebrate and be happy with you?

Let's face it: it's our deep relationships that provide real value in our lives.

A friend who stays up late listening to you talk about a break-up or a business fiasco is priceless — as is one who truly shares your joy at a time of great happiness. And there's nothing like knowing that you're as priceless to others as they are to you — the "go-to" person, the one they turn to first in certain situations.

When you develop bonds like these with other people, you

become infinitely valuable resources for each other, not just connected nodes in a social network. Remember the "spheres of resource and influence" we talked about in the previous chapter? Bonds like these make you part of each others' *Orbits*, which extend the support you provide for each other into a wider, more powerful support structure. The value you provide for each other can extend outward, to and from others with whom both of you are connected.

Creating this support structure isn't as simple as clicking on invitations to "friend" or connect with others online. It takes some effort. But making that effort can be immensely worthwhile.

Let's look at some examples of real-life Orbits, and at the valuable benefits that strong bonds can provide.

The Chinese Principle of Guanxi

One of the most striking examples of the Orbit phenomenon we've noticed is in Chinese business culture. Here's Max's description of his first encounter with it:

> In 1993, we opened the Asia Pacific headquarters for the ISIS Papyrus Group in Singapore. Singapore has four major racial groups as inhabitants, but the Chinese are in the driver's seat in terms of business. Having hired a Chinese local manager, we learned very quickly about the Chinese business principle of "Guanxi." While the word literally means "relationships," its meaning in the Chinese business world is more like, "You scratch my back, I'll scratch yours."
>
> Guanxi minimizes the risks, barriers, and amount of bureaucratic red tape involved when you're doing business in China or with Chinese business people

elsewhere in the world. Because Guanxi can sometimes be misused and lead to corruption, the Singapore government has been very strict in applying its anti-corruption guidelines.

Chinese business people nurture Guanxi religiously in their business networks, in time-intensive ways. They visit the homes of their partners to greet the family and bring gifts, and they devote time to learning more about their partners — as they expect their partners to do for them. People who can assist their partners in solving problems are said to have "good Guanxi."

Chinese business people generally do business first with trusted friends. In China, as well as in Taiwan, you can't expect to walk into a new business and leave with a signed contract, even if your product is both the best and the cheapest on the market. If you haven't worked to build a relationship long before the sale, you'll get only a friendly "Sorry." On the other hand, if you've taken time to prove your honesty and dependability—both essential components of a Guanxi relationship — you're likely to walk away with a contract *and* a valuable business connection.

Because Guanxi is built on strong, well-nurtured bonds, it creates more than just a person-to-person network of contacts. It creates spheres of resource and influence — Orbits — that support those within these spheres as they help each other achieve their goals.

Politics Built on Personal Relationships

Powerful world leaders might not seem like people who need to nurture their relationships in order to achieve their goals. If you look at the most successful ones, though, you're likely to find that they understood the value of having strong Orbits.

Take Sir Winston Churchill, for example. Most people think of him as an influential war leader, which he certainly was as British prime minister during World War II. But many don't realize how much of his influence came from the effort he put into maintaining strong relationships with other leaders and a diverse group of friends.

At one point, Churchill devoted much of his energy trying to persuade United States President Franklin Roosevelt to support him in the war. A master at using frequent communication to build depth of relationships, Churchill wrote the president several letters and established a strong connection with him.

Churchill didn't just interact with the president in a business setting, as many of us do when we're trying to achieve a strategic goal. He made a point of going deeper and developing a personal relationship — one built on a foundation of friendship and trust. As a result, he managed to get American help in the Atlantic, where Britain's lifeline to the New World had been under continual threat from German U-Boats.

Churchill had allies in other Orbits as well. At the same time that he was attempting to build a strong alliance with the United States, Churchill sent aid to the Soviet Union and defended Joseph Stalin in public. "If Hitler invaded Hell," he said, "I would at least make a favorable reference to the Devil in the House of Commons."

Among others in Churchill's personal and professional Orbits were Charlie Chaplin, Albert Einstein, Professor Frederick Lindemann (the first Viscount Cherwell, who became his scientific advisor), and Aristotle Onassis. He had a wide array of friends, across various nations, industries, and avocations.

Churchill knew that creating strong ties with others was well worth the time he put into it. His ability to pick up the phone, call someone, and make something important happen came not just from his position of power, but also from the credibility and trust he had built into his relationships — the strength of his Orbits.

The Importance of "Social Capital"

Remember the old adage, "It's not what you know, but who you know"? In today's fast-food-friend nation, many people seem to have forgotten it. However, as the concept of Guanxi acknowledges—and as examples like that of Churchill show — it's advice well worth remembering.

When you put time and effort into maintaining strong relationships, you're creating something of value. Among those who study social networks — a group that includes sociologists, social psychologists, anthropologists, biologists, economists, information scientists, and business-organization specialists — that value is called "social capital." To define it more precisely, social capital is the value that individuals get from or deliver to the network.

The business person providing resources to colleagues, getting to know them as people, and helping them solve problems is creating social capital, as is the political leader who forges personal connections and builds trust with leaders of other countries. They are creating a valuable asset on which they can draw later, when they are the ones in need of resources or support.

Too often, people see social capital solely in terms of what they can get *from* a social network, rather than what they deliver *to* the network. However, when they haven't forged strong bonds with the others in that network — when they haven't created Orbits — they haven't created much in the way of social capital at all. The incentive for others to provide resources and support to them is relatively low, because they haven't provided such value to others. They've failed to see that social capital is both an asset and a responsibility.

When you view the strong bonds you forge with people as an investment in social capital, the value you're creating in terms of resources and support seems more tangible, more worth the effort. But there's even more reason to create strong bonds when you look at a less tangible side: the emotional rewards.

Happiness is Contagious

During our discussion of the idea of Orbits as "spheres of resource and influence," did the word "influence" make you think of political or social power used to achieve goals? Well, there's also another, more unconscious type of influence that works strongly within Orbits and larger social networks: emotional influence — particularly happiness.

You might not be aware of it, but the influence of people you interact with each day affects your emotional cycle. The friendly smile of the booth agent at the transit station might become a simple but regular element of each day that you suddenly miss when it isn't there. The grouchiness of the man at the newspaper stand might be something that entertains you each morning. And your partner's outlook at breakfast might affect your mood — and the moods of the other people you deal with — all day long.

This type of influence may not seem like such a good thing when you first contemplate it. After all, other people's emotional influences might just as easily be negative as positive, right?

Actually, a study by James H. Fowler and Nicholas A. Christakis, based on 20 years of emotion-evaluating surveys from a large social network, shows that our happiness — more than our unhappiness — depends on the happiness of others to whom we're connected. As Fowler and Christakis put it: "The number of happy friends seems to have a more reliable effect on ego happiness than the number of unhappy friends."

Not only did they find evidence for contagious happiness, they found it to flow beyond friends to "friends of friends," and even to a third degree of separation (friends of one's friends' friends.) Not surprisingly, in light of that finding, they found that people near the center of a social network tended to be happier than those on the periphery.

They also found the happiness influence to be measurably greater for stronger, more reciprocal friendships (those in which both people listed each other as being friends) than for weaker, more one-sided friendships (in which one person named the other as a friend, but not vice versa).

So, when you invest in strong relationships, you're not just building social capital; you're also creating more potential for happiness — a "happiness dividend," of sorts.

Friends With *Real* Benefits

When you realize the benefits of strong relationships — resources, support, the "happiness dividend," and having an Orbit of people who value you and matter to you — the question of whether you should invest some effort in maintaining such relationships seems like a no-brainer.

The obvious next questions, of course, are: What makes relationships strong? And how do you know when your relationship bonds become strong enough to create an Orbit?

We'll address both of those questions in the next chapter.

 **CHAPTER THREE**

What Makes Relationships Strong— and Orbital

Who are the people closest to you? Take a moment to picture them: the people who make up both your personal and your professional "support networks." They're the ones who are there for you when you need them, and who turn to you in similar situations.

If you had to make a list of them, it wouldn't be difficult. You know who they are.

If you had to describe what *makes* these particular relationships so strong, though, you might not find it quite so easy. What characteristics do these relationships share? What factors contribute to their strength?

These are questions worth thinking about. The more you understand about what makes a relationship strong, the better equipped you are to create strong relationships — and sustaining Orbits — with the people around you.

The Four Components of Relationship Strength

Let's take a moment to explore relationships from the perspective of a sociologist. In 1973, the influential sociologist Mark Granovetter proposed that the strength of a relationship between two individuals in a social network was related to the amount of time, emotional intensity, intimacy (mutual confiding), and reciprocal services involved in the relationship. Or, to use the slightly punchier version of this idea expressed by social-media scientist Michael Wu …

We can assess relationship strength by looking at the strength of the following four components:

- Time

- Intensity

- Trust

- Reciprocity

In other words, a stronger bond is generally one created over a greater amount of time, with more intensity, more trust, more reciprocity, or more of all these components built into it. Viewing relationship strength from this perspective gives us better insight into how to strengthen the bonds we build with others, both in business and in life.

Let's take a deeper look at how each of these components contributes to relationship strength.

Time: Being Present and Attentive

The most significant gift you can give to a relationship is time. When you don't spend time with the other person, there's no chance to develop intensity, trust, or reciprocity. Time is a unique and totally unrepeatable gift. It costs nothing but is extremely scarce, because it can be spent only once.

If you spend an hour around a large dinner table with 10 other people, does that count as an hour spent on each relationship? Good try, but no. What you can and should be giving to a relationship you want to strengthen is *attentive* time: time spent directly engaged with the other person. The more exclusive and undivided your attention during that time, the better.

You're better off spending about six minutes in one-on-one conversation with each of those 10 folks at the dinner than talking to all 10 across the table for an hour — especially if your focus in each individual conversation is on listening to the other person. Listening is an important part of giving someone your attention, and trying to understand that person's perspective will do more to strengthen your relationship than would simply airing your perspective.

We also believe that time you spend on maintaining a relationship — even when you're not in the other person's presence — contributes to the relationship's strength. When you spend time doing someone a favor, picking out a card or gift for that person, or writing him or her a note, you're putting time and attention into the relationship. (Remember the saying, "It's the thought that counts"? Thought is certainly a form of attentive time.) While this effort is no substitute for time spent in someone's presence, it can be an important addition to that time.

Intensity: The Emotional Connection

When your connection with someone is emotionally intense, the potential for a strong relationship is clearly there. Remember our comparison of emotional connections to gravitational forces pulling planets into orbit? Emotion is the connecting force in every Orbit you have. It determines whether you feel a "pull" toward another person, and it dictates whether that person is drawn toward an orbital relationship with you.

Spending time with someone one-on-one and face-to-face provides more opportunity for an intense connection than you get in groups (where the connection is diluted) and in virtual encounters. As humans, we are all driven by feelings and emotions linked to the patterns of our five senses. When you interact with someone in person, you communicate on multiple "channels." Eye contact, vocal nuances, body language, scent, and touch all play their parts in shaping the messages you exchange and intensifying the emotional connection.

Of course, not all emotional connections are positive. Attitude is important in guiding the intensity of your connections with others in a positive direction, as we'll discuss later in this chapter.

Trust: Earned Over Time

In a strong and authentic relationship, there's always a basis of trust — that is, the belief of the people in the relationship that they can rely on each other. Trust is not usually granted instantly. Rather, it is earned over time.

By demonstrating your reliability to another person, you earn that person's trust. Each time you prove yourself reliable, the trust becomes stronger. And any time you prove yourself unreliable, you damage that trust — sometimes irrevocably.

In business relationships, trust is often built through reliable products, service, and follow-through on promises. For example, if you have a tire blowout on the road and need a new tire to continue, you might end up buying it from an unfamiliar tire business near the site of your blowout — one you don't know whether you can trust, so you just hope for the best. You may think you're simply having a one-time encounter. However, if that tire business delivers on the top-level service it claims to offer, and if its tire lives up to its product guarantees, the business will start to earn your trust. Over time, if it continues to deliver on those promises, it may become the business you go to for all your tire needs.

In personal relationships, earning trust is a much more private matter. While part of how you earn another person's trust is by behaving reliably — being there when you say you will, doing what you say you'll do, and in other ways demonstrating your honesty — another major aspect of how you build trust is by protecting the other person's privacy. When someone confides in you and you refrain from sharing the information with others, you are building a foundation of trust for your relationship. Similarly, when a friend does something that he or she would prefer not be widely known about, refraining from telling others is an important way to show that you are trustworthy.

Putting too much out there for the world to see can be perceived as a violation of trust. The more you divulge private information from your relationship to another person, the less personal that relationship becomes.

On the other hand, the more you demonstrate that you can keep private information confidential, the more trust you can build with others. The secrets you share with another person can turn out to be the strongest bond in your relationship.

Reciprocity: A Mutual Choice

Like trust, reciprocity is not something you can demand from a relationship. When two people choose to engage in a reciprocal give-and-take that benefits them both, they build strength and value into their relationship. But when one person gives, and the other doesn't want to take — or the other person takes, but doesn't give back — the relationship will necessarily be a weaker one. And if it's entirely one-sided, it won't be part of your Orbits.

When we described what Orbits are, in Chapter 1, we emphasized that the people in your Orbits are connected to you by reciprocal bonds, and we noted that they take on roles that balance and resonate with yours. If the giving is all one-way, there is no balance. And if the roles you allow each other to play in your lives aren't complementary, there may not even be a significant relationship between the two of you.

We use the word "allow" here because the role you play in any relationship can never be greater than what the other person permits — and the permission will be based on how that person perceives you, not on how you perceive yourself. If you view yourself as someone's friend, but he or she views you merely as an acquaintance, the two of you are not playing complementary roles in each others' lives.

We don't always realize how different other people's perceptions of our roles may be, as this story from Max shows:

> In college we had a young, really interesting Catholic priest who taught religious history classes. He was kind of a maverick who wore jeans, a thick violet sweater, and a huge gold cross around his neck. At the time, that was too radical for much of the faculty, but the students loved it.
>
> He taught me a huge amount about human relationships. The first part was when he drew a relationship matrix of our class. Each person had to write on a piece of paper who we liked the most and who we liked the least. No one knew that he would make the information public. We were shocked when he pulled out the classroom

seating chart and we saw that he'd drawn arrows on it that showed the likes and dislikes of each student. He then pointed out that my relationships were the most interesting. I could see why.

There weren't that many people who liked me, and the person I liked the most actually liked me the least. He was an immensely fit young guy who was always one of the best students in class. He was quiet, intelligent, and polite, and he had never said anything negative to me. I was one of the worst students — boasting and overbearing, trying to be accepted by others while still being kind of a loner and keeping to myself.

We were both surprised to see our strange situation, because neither of us had known about it. We realized that we hadn't really bothered to work out a relationship. Being hit over the head with this fact helped us turn our non-relationship into a friendship.

While you can't make another person perceive you in the way you want to be perceived — or insist that someone reciprocate what you offer — it's still important to offer what you can to others. If you approach them with a "them-centric" attitude, showing them what you are willing to give them *without expecting something in return*, you can demonstrate the value that a relationship with you would offer.

It may seem paradoxical that the way to encourage reciprocal relationships would be to give without expecting anything back, but think about this: If someone does you a favor but then seems to be expecting a favor in return, how do you feel? If you feel pressured to reciprocate, does that give you a positive impression of the other person, or a negative one?

On the other hand, if someone does you a favor and seems

genuinely pleased to help you, with no other motivation or expectation, would your impression be more positive? You might even feel a spontaneous urge to reciprocate. You might not, but there's a good chance you'd still be left with a positive feeling toward that person.

If you choose to give to others without expectation, you won't be disappointed when your doing so doesn't lead to anything. But your willingness to give and share will most likely have a positive effect, and when it generates reciprocal efforts in others, you'll experience the pleasure of stronger bonds and expanded Orbits.

Positively Strong: The Orbital Bond

The four components we've discussed — time, intensity, trust, and reciprocity — are vitally important for building strong relationships. But are they the only four components needed to make those relationships orbital?

You can spend a fair amount of time with someone without forming an orbital connection — even if your interactions are intense and involve some level of trust and reciprocity. Intensity can be negative; trust and reciprocity can be strategic, rather than heartfelt; and time spent with someone uncomfortable to be around can make the relationship strongly negative instead of positive.

So, all four of these components combined are insufficient without one more ingredient: consideration. By "consideration," we mean behaving kindly, with regard for each other's feelings. Or, to use the language of the Golden Rule, treating others as you would like to be treated.

Consideration is essential for creating bonds that are not only strong, but positive. These strong, positive bonds are exactly what you need to connect you with others in the supportive spheres of resource and influence that constitute your Orbits. Because you are strongly connected to the others in your Orbits, you can influence each other in a meaningful way. And because your connections are based on trust, reciprocity, and consideration, you know you can depend on each other as valuable resources in each other's lives.

Now that you know what it takes to create orbital relationships, what's getting in your way? Plenty, as it turns out — that's the topic of our next chapter.

CHAPTER FOUR

What's Grounding Your Orbits

Now that you know what characterizes strong, orbital relationships, take a moment to picture a situation that's becoming increasingly common in today's world: four people sit together at a restaurant table — two men and two women, let's say — without talking for minutes at a time; all are engrossed in looking at their smartphones.

Are they devoting attentive time to one another? Interacting intensely and developing trust? Engaging in any kind of reciprocal give-and-take? Showing each other basic courtesy and consideration? Are they, in short, building their Orbits?

Not with each other. And, even though they're probably interacting with other people via email or social media, there's a good chance they're not building orbital relationships with those folks at the moment, either.

"But why?" you may ask. "Isn't it possible that they're bonding with other people on their smartphones and building Orbits that way?"

Possible, yes — but not likely, unless they're making a conscious effort to "buck the tide" of prevailing practices. Too many features of today's internet-relationship culture tend to work *against* building strong bonds, instead of *toward* doing so.

Consider this headline of a recent article in the *Silicon Valley / San Jose Business Journal*: "Facebook 'friends' cause stress, anxiety." The article quotes psychologist Kathy Charles, leader of a study at Edinburgh Napier University on the effects of Facebook use, as saying that, "We found it was actually those with the most contacts, those who had invested the most time in the site, who were the ones most likely to be stressed." The study identified several causes of tension among Facebook users, including etiquette worries, pressure to be inventive and entertaining, and fear of missing something important when logged out.

Hmm… doesn't sound like these folks are building a lot of social capital through Facebook. They may be gaining other benefits from their hyper-connectedness, but it seems like they're not experiencing much of a "happiness dividend."

Let's take a closer look at how aspects of today's culture are getting in the way of creating orbital relationships and fulfilling the potential that social networks can offer. Specifically, let's look at what's working against the ability to build relationships through time, intensity, trust, reciprocity, and consideration.

Time: A Key Limiting Factor

As you'll recall from our discussion of time as a relationship-strengthening force, what you really need to invest in relationships is attentive time. And let's face it: your attentive time is a limited resource now more than ever. With smart phones, laptops, and tablets becoming more and more a part of our lives, we often find ourselves splitting our attention between the people (and events) around us and the constant stream of email messages and social-media posts linking us to far-flung others through our devices.

Business strategists such as Thomas H. Davenport and J.C. Beck have been talking for over a decade about how we now live in an "attention economy." As Davenport noted in 2001, "Through research and simple observation, I've become convinced that attention is *the* scarce resource in today's economy."

As we try to split our time and attention among an ever-widening array of social and professional contacts, the amount available per person gets smaller and smaller. Plus, our available attention for others is limited not just by the fixed number of hours in a day, but also by our brains' limited ability to juggle social relationships with more than a certain number of people.

In fact, that "certain number" — the number of people with whom we can mentally manage social bonds simultaneously — has actually been identified by various scientists. They don't all agree on a single number, but they aren't too far apart, either.

A commonly cited value for this number — proposed by anthropologist Robin Dunbar in the 1990s — is 148, often rounded to 150. Dunbar determined this number based on a relationship he discovered between the neocortex ratio of a given primate species (the ratio between the size of the neocortex and the size of the brain) and the typical size of that species' social groups. When he plugged the neocortex ratio for humans into his equation, it predicted a social group size of about 148. (Some researchers following Dunbar have suggested much higher numbers — 291, for example — as being a more typical network size at the start of the 21st century, but in the absence of any increased processing power in our brains, we question whether they're describing *sustainable* relationships.)

Dunbar has found confirmation of his predicted group size in such varied groups as hunter-gatherer societies, military-fighting units, and religious communities. Recently, he has even found it in virtual worlds such as Second Life and World of Warcraft.

What does this number mean in our day-to-day lives? As Dunbar explains it, there are only so many people with whom we can have a two-way relationship with some history attached to it. Basically, these are the people whom "you wouldn't feel embarrassed about joining if you happened to find them in the bar in the transit lounge of Hong Kong airport at 3 a.m." He notes that our social world tends to hit a limit when it reaches 150 people: "What seems to set the limit at 150 — the outer layer [of the social network] — is that you run out of time and psychological capital to give to more people."

So, even though the ease of connecting with people on Facebook and other social-media sites may seem to offer unlimited friendship possibilities, this apparent lack of limits is an illusion. Any attempt to create strong, orbital relationships needs to confront the very real limits posed by time, our increasingly distracted attention, and the finite capacity of our brains.

Ultimately, because we can't create or extend it, time is the most valuable resource we can give to a relationship.

Intensity: Lessening As We Communicate in More Ways

Think for a moment about the tremendous variety of ways you can communicate with others today:

• Face-to-face physical meetings, either one-on-one or in a group

• Snail mail

• Phone calls (often made and received on the go, sometimes with headsets)

- Text messages

- Email (accessible not just on your desktop computer, but also on your laptop, tablet, or smartphone)

- Social media posts, comments, and messages

- Video conferencing

Now, think about which of these communication methods allow you to make the most intense emotional connections with others. Are smileys and other emoticons as effective as real smiles, vocal nuances, and body-language signals? Are video conferences as intense as physical meetings, which provide extra dimensions of touch, fully visible body language, and scent? (Keep in mind the strong connection that scent has to our emotions and memories — it may not be the *most* important way we connect, as it is with many animals, but it can still contribute to the intensity of any face-to-face encounter.) Finally, can a Facebook post or a tweet sent to you and scores of others ever approach the emotional intensity of a communication meant for you alone?

True, some of these methods give us more communicative context than we had back in the days of telephone and telegraph only. For example, multi-person video conferences give us more levels of communication — with more potential for emotional intensity — than were available with just conference calls. And, of course, we still have face-to-face meetings as an option.

But it seems as though the ease of alternate communication methods often makes them a substitute for the more intense option of face-to-face meetings. And these days, even when you're communicating with someone in person in a one-on-one situation, the intensity can easily be disrupted by a cell-phone call, a text message, or an email notification from some third party.

Clearly, the distancing effect of many of today's communication methods is another obstacle we need to address in regaining relationship intensity and building strong Orbits.

Trust: Difficult to Build Without Privacy

As more and more of us become accustomed to communicating and sharing personal information through social media — essentially trusting an audience of many with intimate details of our lives — the notion of trust starts to lose its meaning. If someone says, "I trust you," but you know that person also trusts everyone else, that trust is no big deal.

Similarly, if information is revealed to a large number of people at once, its value is discounted. We found it funny that CNN came up with this slogan for its news: "Be the first to know!" Well, sure, if "first" means "first at the same moment with a few million people around the globe." News that is shared widely isn't truly valuable. It loses its value both as a scarce commodity and also as a means for bonding with others when shared confidentially.

In the previous chapter, we discussed how real trust is earned over time. You earn another person's trust by repeatedly showing that you are reliable and that you can keep confidential information private. But how can you show yourself trustworthy if most or all of your interactions with the other person are public — for example, on a Facebook page?

If you don't have truly private interactions with another person, the two of you never have the opportunity to exchange confidences. And since you don't share information privately, you lose the chance to show that you can be trusted to keep the information private. Plus, if you communicate one-on-one but not in person — for example, by email only — you lose the nonverbal signals such as eye contact and handshakes that help to reinforce an intuitive sense of trust.

People who have fully embraced the idea of living their lives in public tend to dismiss worries about privacy loss as being outdated. "Public is the new private," some say, with the implication that we all need to get used to the change. Youth Radio reporter Lauren Silverman, in her 2008 commentary on the topic, noted that, among her under-25 age group, "communicating with friends through private channels has become unheard of, even passé." But she also admitted that she sometimes longed for "the good old days when people knew *me*, rather than my Facebook profile" — and that she was "still quietly debating whether public is in fact *better* than private."

As Facebook moves toward making more of the personal information you put on its site available to others beyond your Friend lists, you may well feel a loss of trust. But consider what else you may have lost by broadcasting your personal information widely: the ability to share that information meaningfully with selected people to build trust — and to build Orbits of strong relationships.

Reciprocity: A Lost Art in a One-Way Culture

Remember when you first realized how little you had to do to maintain social-media relationships? If you were used to receiving more email than you could easily keep up with, you may have been pleasantly surprised by the one-way nature of most Facebook communications. "Look at all those posts and comments I *don't* have to respond to! I can read them when I have time — and ignore them when I don't!"

Status messages are basically broadcasts to an audience of friends. We may send them to subgroups of only certain friends (say, using Facebook's "Close Friends" list, or one of its other Friend Lists or Smart Lists), but they're still broadcasts if they go to more than one person. Even a post on a friend's wal l—which is, in theory, a message directly to that friend — is a public message, delivered in front of an audience, with the friend not even present. While a response is a nice gesture, it's not strictly required.

When we get used to the one-sided nature of Facebook messages, we may well find ourselves sometimes not responding even to Facebook's version of email — that is, messages sent one-on-one in a more private manner. (Whether they are truly private is questionable, given Facebook's inclination to own any information we provide on the site). In fact, we may find ourselves less inclined to respond even to email messages we receive *outside* of Facebook; they can start to seem like they are simply additional shout-outs floating by on the stream of one-way messages that scroll by us all day from Facebook, LinkedIn, Twitter, and other sources.

We may find ourselves getting into the habit of "me-centric," one-way thinking — and out of the habit of reciprocating the considerate gestures of others. Those of us who take in posts and tweets without responding to them may feel less need to respond to the favors others do for us in our daily lives. Those of us who like to post and tweet to our audience may come to expect that others will listen to us offline as well, without our needing to give them the gift of our attention in return.

As we discussed in the previous chapter, the type of reciprocity that characterizes strong relationships and sustaining Orbits can't be demanded of others. Instead, we must nudge it forward by giving to others without expectation.

By demonstrating thoughtfulness toward others, we can encourage them to respond thoughtfully to us, and thus to grow a reciprocal relationship of mutual value. By keeping their confidential information private, for example, we encourage them to do the same for us. And by being there when they need us — even when it means answering a call in the middle of the night—we encourage them to be there when we need them.

We need to remember, though, that developing two-way relationships takes extra effort — and extra consideration—in an increasingly one-way world.

Consideration: More Challenging and More Necessary

As we connect in more distant ways — online or through devices, in ways that are often not one-on-one or face-to-face — we may find ourselves becoming less considerate of others without realizing it. The same friend whose greeting on the street we would never fail to acknowledge might greet us on Facebook and get no response. We might avoid interrupting the conversations of others when we are with them and yet think nothing of answering a text while they are talking — or of expecting them to drop everything when we phone or text them. We may never shout at strangers in real life (other than in dangerous situations) yet find ourselves using the textual equivalent (EVERY LETTER CAPITALIZED!) in participating in a comment thread online with people we don't know.

The scarcity of our available time also affects our ability to be considerate, in the sense that consideration means considering others. It means taking the time to include others in our contemplations and to think about how to be there for them. With less time in our schedules, even taking a few moments to think about others can seem like a luxury, rather than a necessity. In fact, though, this type of consideration is a necessity for building strong relationships.

Basically, the same aspects of today's communication methods that challenge our efforts to strengthen our relationships also challenge our efforts to treat each other with respect and consideration — making it even more necessary that we try to do so.

Building Our Orbits in Challenging Circumstances

As we've seen in this chapter, there is a downside to the amazing, 24/7 connectedness we now have to a wide range of people through social media and mobile devices. While this situation has created unprecedented opportunities for global networking and the exchange of information and ideas, it has also produced a set of circumstances that works against our ability to create strong relationships and sustain Orbits.

The circumstances grounding our Orbits include the following:

- **Less Time:** The ease of relationship creation through social media encourages us to split our time and attention too many ways — and among more relationships than our brains can comfortably manage.

- **Less Intensity:** Because we now connect in many ways that are neither face-to-face nor one-on-one, the intensity of our relationships is diminished.

- **Less Trust:** As more of our interactions with others become public, instead of private, we lose the ability to exchange confidences and build trust by keeping each other's information private.

- **Less Reciprocity:** The one-way nature of many social-media messages gets us out of the habit of reciprocating each other's communications and kind gestures.

- **Less Consideration:** Communicating in ways that are more distant and not face-to-face makes rudeness easier — and more important to avoid.

So, while our lives today are more connected to the lives of others, the circumstances in which we conduct these relationships challenge our ability to strengthen them and develop our Orbits.

Fortunately, the insights you've gained into the nature of strong relationships will help you to meet that challenge when you combine those insights with the strategies we'll discuss in the next two chapters.

CHAPTER FIVE

Connecting Strongly With Others

At some point, you may realize that the number of "friends" in your social networks doesn't mean nearly as much as it could. Too many of them are so distantly acquainted that your connection brings no discernible benefits or joy to either you or them.

Let's say you decide you aren't satisfied with an ever-expanding network of social-media contacts who barely know you. You'd like to create strong connections instead of weak ones. You're ready to build your Orbits–your "spheres of resource and influence" — and leverage the untapped potential of your social networks.

You are ready to invest in relationships. But how do you counteract the lowered expectations of the current fast-food-friends culture?

You can start by remembering this: Reciprocity is essential. Not only is it one of the vital components of strong relationships, it's also the *key* component when it comes to establishing a strong connection. If the other person isn't interested in deepening the relationship, it will go nowhere, regardless of the time you devote to it.

Creating a relationship of value with another person ultimately requires effort from both of you — which means you need to establish a real connection, one that motivates the other person to respond. Keep in mind that you are asking that person for some time and attention, our scarcest resources in today's "attention economy." To be deemed worthy of another person's time and attention, you need to stand out from the background noise — from the stream of emails, tweets, and status updates that bombard that person daily.

So, what will make you stand out and motivate another person to respond to you? Establishing a positive emotional connection. In other words, bringing in intensity and consideration, two other elements that we've seen are necessary to strong relationships.

"Wait," you may say, "An emotional connection with someone isn't something you can create if it's not there. Either it happens or it doesn't."

That's absolutely right. You can't control how other people feel about you. But you *can* determine the attitude and approach you bring to potential relationships — and those aspects of how you reach out to others can make all the difference.

What attitude and approach are we talking about? Before we get to specific suggestions, let's look at some real-life examples from two areas that may at first seem far removed from your life and relationships, but that offer important lessons: international diplomacy and sales.

Diligent Diplomacy: Making Moments Matter

If you're a high-ranking public official of a powerful country, does it really matter whether you connect on a personal level with leaders of other countries? Judging from the immense efforts Hillary Clinton and her staff make, according to a recent documentary, the answer is a resounding yes.

The documentary "Inside the State Department" chronicles a year in which Secretary of State Clinton traveled to 50 countries, yet still managed to orchestrate an immense amount of research and planning to personalize each meeting with a foreign leader — including choosing an appropriate gift for that leader from the State Department's "gift vault."

The gift vault is an enormous storage facility full of one-of-a-kind gifts, such as sports equipment autographed by famous athletes, unique works of art, and items donated by renowned authors or associated with important historical figures. State Department staffers select each gift only after careful research into the intended recipient's likes and dislikes. Why? They understand the importance of establishing a positive personal connection.

Even more important than the thoughtfully chosen gifts are the circumstances in which they're presented: the face-to-face meetings that dictated Clinton's demanding 50-country travel schedule during the year the documentary was made. Meeting with other leaders face-to-face gave her the chance to connect with them emotionally and create the basis for a strong relationship, as she explains in the film:

"It's not just quantity of travel, but also quality of travel. It's hard to explain why you have to keep going back over and over again [to meet the same people]. But people want to look you in the eye, get some sense of your humanity, as they want to know if they can trust you and therefore trust your country. It's a day-by-day investment of the time it takes to try to get the results for our country. Moments matter, as it is a way of connecting with people."

Clinton goes on to explain why it's imperative to make every effort — even in seemingly small ways — to bridge the gaps between cultures and connect with other world leaders: "It's rare that you get one 'big bang' moment in diplomacy. If we are moving in the right direction, I'll take an inch — because that inch can be built on to become a foot, then a yard, and a mile."

An attitude that emotional connections "either happen or they don't" wouldn't go far in bridging the gaps in international diplomacy. That's why Clinton and her staff do everything they can to encourage those connections to happen. They learn as much as they can in advance about the leaders they'll be meeting, choose gifts that convey personal consideration, and travel extensively to create the face-to-face meeting conditions that provide maximum intensity and trust-building opportunities.

Your life may not involve creating strategic alliances between countries, but anyone building relationships —a nd Orbits — can learn from Clinton's example. Diligent preparation, personal consideration, and private, face-to-face meeting conditions go a long way toward creating a positive emotional connection

Now let's look at an example from another profession in which success can depend greatly on relationship-building skills: sales. Like diplomacy, it offers important lessons about how to connect strongly with others.

Sales-School Lesson #1: Competing for Attention

Let's say you're *not* the chief diplomat of an extremely powerful country. In this case, you probably have a more basic challenge to confront before you can start bridging the gaps between you and others: getting their attention.

Remember our discussion of the "attention economy"? Attention is a scarce resource not only for you, but also for the people with whom you want to connect. In seeking some of their time and attention, you're inevitably going to find yourself competing with everyone else who's seeking the same thing.

So, even if you don't think of yourself as a salesperson — in fact, even if the thought of trying to sell anything makes you break out in hives — you must confront the same question every salesperson does: How do I stand out from the competition? How do I persuade others to spend some of their limited resources — time and attention — on what I am offering? In this case, of course, what you are offering is a relationship, rather than a product or a "solution," but the basic question is the same. And if the question is the same, some of the answers may be, too.

For some insights in the area of standing out from the competition, let's hear a story from Mike's years as a Marketing Representative for IBM:

I had a newly-assigned prospecting territory, meaning I could call on any company within my geographical assignment, as long as it wasn't already an existing IBM customer.

> Driving home on a Friday afternoon, I suddenly came upon a large retail establishment. Given how far I was from home, it wasn't likely that I might return to this area any time soon. So, I decided to stop in. Following my IBM training, I asked courteously if I could speak to the Executive Assistant to the CEO.

> A well-dressed and imposing woman came to greet me and inquired why I wished to speak to Mr. X. After first saying, as taught, that I was "your" IBM Marketing Rep and apologizing that I came unannounced, I said I was hoping to introduce myself to the CEO and see

if he might like to set up a future meeting to explore what IBM had successfully been doing within "your" industry (the "your" part was simply a means to achieve a more personal connection).

She asked for my business card and went to into the CEO's office. Out came a handsome man with a commanding appearance. We shook hands, I went through my IBM spiel again, and this is what I remember him saying: "Well, I would actually be very interested in hearing more of what you want to say, but I'm getting ready to leave for a skiing vacation in Colorado with my family. I'll be returning in two weeks, so please feel free to contact me afterwards." After exchanging a few more words with him, I went back to my car.

Now, this was well before the internet and the PC, so I entered in my DayTimer a note to call him in three weeks, wanting to give him time to settle back in after his family holiday. "Ask him how his family skiing vacation in Colorado went," I wrote.

Three weeks later I phoned him, greeting his Executive Assistant by her name (which I had made sure to ask and jot down in my notes) when she answered. She connected me to the CEO, to whom I identified myself by my name and "your IBM Marketing Rep."

The next words out of my mouth were, "Mr. X, how was your skiing vacation with your family in Colorado?"

After what seemed like a full minute of silence, he said, "Mike, you're probably a pretty smart guy, working for IBM. So, you may have guessed that your competition has also been trying to meet with me. In fact, I encountered them a few weeks ago and said the same thing to them that I did to you."

I wasn't sure where he was going with this, so I remained silent as he continued, "I had also had mentioned to them that I was going on a family skiing vacation in Colorado. Since my return, they have already contacted me, and you are the last to do so."

Uh-oh, here it comes, I thought.

"But do you know that you are the only one who remembered to ask me how my holiday went? What that tells me is that you paid attention to me and considered everything I said to be important. That, to me, is the difference between a professional and an amateur. I like to deal with professionals — so, yes, I would be very interested in setting up a meeting with you."

Whew! I went on to create another IBM customer — and to develop the deep appreciation for relationships that eventually led me to co-invent two relationship-management software products.

It may seem strange that such a small moment of courteous personal attention could make such a big difference, but it did. As Hillary Clinton put it: "moments matter." In sales, as in diplomacy, a few moments spent focusing personal attention on others in a considerate way can spark crucial emotional connections — connections that make you stand out and that motivate others to invite you into their Orbits.

What we're talking about, ultimately, is being detail-oriented in your approach and "them-centric" in your attitude. A detail-oriented approach is one that involves noticing and remembering details about other people that are essential to who they are, like the Executive Assistant's name and Mr. X's making a family ski vacation a priority. And a them-centric attitude toward others is one that involves you paying attention to *them* — to their human interests and needs, like the need to be recognized as a unique individual. Being them-centric also means being attuned to the other person's comfort and relaxation, creating an atmosphere in which your relationship can flourish.

Sales-School Lesson #2: Getting Personal

To enlarge our picture of a them-centric approach in action, let's hear one more story of Mike's sales background helping him to make a personal connection:

> When I was in sales school training at IBM, they taught us a technique called "What's On The Walls?" If you go to a person's office, it's rare not to see items on their desk or shelves — or hung on the walls — that represent some of their strongest interests. Pictures of family, especially kids or grandkids, are likely, as are pictures of time spent in recreational activities, such as boating or golfing. So are university diplomas, certificates of honor, participation reminders of charitable events, special-interest magazines, and so on. People like to talk about what they enjoy, so asking about these items is a good way to relax them and make your encounter more memorable.
>
> A while back, I was in another country visiting some high-level executives in an organization, and I mentioned that I was attempting to meet a particular Country Manager of a Fortune 1000 company with whom I could envision a relationship of mutual benefit. They said they knew him well and had a meeting coming up that I was welcome to attend as a tag-along.
>
> The next day, I accompanied two of them on a visit to

the Country Manager's office. This person's last name lent itself to the nickname he went by, "Goz." When we met, everyone exchanged the usual courtesies. After our introduction, Goz said nothing more to me as we all went into his office. While the three of them talked business for half an hour or so, I discreetly scanned his desk and walls for any sign of a way to "break the ice." Against the background of items representing business accomplishments, one item in particular stood out. It looked like a customized stuffed animal made by a child in an effort to portray Goz — sort of a caricature of his business persona. I can't do it justice with my description, so I'll just say that it was cute, the kind of cute that only children can express.

When my associates concluded their discussions with Goz, they told him I had a perspective of possible strategic value to his organization and asked if he would mind taking a little longer to hear me out. He agreed. Knowing his time with us was almost over, I had a choice: get personal or get business. I immediately chose to get personal. I first thanked him for his time, then politely asked if I could call him by his nickname. After he agreed, I said, "Goz, if you don't mind, before I begin, I've noticed that cute stuffed animal over there seems to be a caricature of you. Would you mind telling me what that is all about?"

His demeanor toward me immediately relaxed, and he laughed heartily. He said, "You know, that has been on my desk for many years, and no one has ever asked me about it before." He went on to describe its background and why he displayed it, and we all found ourselves laughing along with him. At the conclusion of our business discussion, he agreed to provide access to his people and expressed an interest in working together for our mutual benefit. When we left his office, my associates started laughing all over again. They said they couldn't believe what they had just learned about Goz — and they had never before seen him become relaxed so quickly with someone he had just met.

While this anecdote, like the previous one, seems on the surface to be about making sales, both of them are really about connecting with others on a personal level — the key to success in sales, in diplomacy, and in initiating strong relationships in an age of distracted, distant, and shallow "frienditutes."

Now that we've seen a few examples of the type of approach that invites a significant personal connection, let's talk about how you can apply this approach in your own relationships.

Connecting With Others: A Blueprint

Chances are, you don't have a gift vault to supply the perfect token of your esteem for each person with whom you want to connect — or a diligent support staff to research what that perfect gift should be. And you probably haven't had years of sales training to hone your ice-breaking skills. But that's okay. What really matters is your attitude and your approach: being them-centric, attentive to detail, and attuned to opportunities for connecting in a relaxed, personal way.

How do you make this approach work in today's device-cluttered, social-media-dominated world? By sidestepping the negative aspects of today's technology and strategically employing the aspects that can help you toward your goals.

Let's look at some specific suggestions for what you can do before, during, and after you meet with someone you'd like to bring into your Orbits.

Before you get together. If you're about to interact with someone and you'd like to encourage a strong connection, take a few moments to do the following:

- **Research the person's interests.** You may not have the resources of the State Department, but as long as you have an internet connection at hand, you're well-equipped to find out more about your potential Orbit member. The one positive side of "public is the new private" is that you can access people's publicly posted information easily and quickly to help you find potential connecting points. "What's On the Walls?" can become "What's On the Facebook Wall?" (or the LinkedIn profile, Twitter feed, or blog post). By showing a genuine interest in what someone has posted publicly, you can generate a conversation that leads you into a more private and personal connection.

- **Put yourself in a them-centric frame of mind.** Think about what you can offer to the other person, not what you may want to get out of the relationship. Remember, the best way to invite reciprocity is by giving to others without expectation and without pressure. And keep in mind that one of the most valuable gifts you can give is your attention. By asking questions and listening attentively to the answers, you can get to know others better and show them true consideration.

- **Relax.** Since your emotional state can strongly affect how others perceive you, as we discussed in Chapter 2, take a few deep, calming breaths. By getting into a relaxed and confident state of mind, you communicate relaxation to others and make them more receptive to connecting with you.

When you meet up. When you get the opportunity to connect with your potential Orbit member, either in a planned meeting or an unexpected encounter, you can encourage a meaningful connection in the following ways:

- **Opt for one-on-one and in-person.** Choose a one-on-one situation if at all possible (or, if necessary, a *small* group); that way, you can give the other person as much as possible of your undivided attention. Also, try to meet in person, so that you're communicating on as many sensory channels as possible: eye contact, body language, and so on. If meeting in person isn't possible, choose a virtual method that allows more sensory channels, rather than fewer, for a higher-intensity connection. (So, choose a video conference over a phone conference, and a phone conference over a text chat).

- **Use context clues to learn about others.** For clues about the other person's interests, adapt the "What's On the Walls?" method to your meeting situation. If you're in someone's office, look on the walls and the desk. If you're somewhere else, observe what the other person is wearing, carrying, and choosing in the moment. Look for something interesting that you can ask about — it may open the door to who that person really is.

- **Give your full attention.** As much as possible, avoid diverting your attention from the other person to deal with distractions such as cell-phone calls, texts, and emails. While some interruptions can't be ignored — say, a message from your spouse that your kid just broke an arm — ignoring interruptions shows the person you're with that you consider him or her important and deserving of your attention. It's better to put yourself in a situation where your interaction can't be easily interrupted — say, by turning off unnecessary devices or closing your office door when you're meeting with someone — than to give people only a slice of your attention when you're trying to connect with them. Max learned this lesson the hard way from the interruptions brought on by his open-door policy: "I noticed that most people would rather I send them away with the promise of a later meeting than give them less than my full attention."

• **Prompt laughter.** As we saw in the Goz story, laughter is a great way to "break the ice" with someone. Try to get the other person to laugh early on, so you relax the encounter and create a positive connection.

• **Be authentic.** Don't act like someone you're not — say, pretending to like what other people like—to try and make them see you a certain way. Acting will only make you less believable and less authentic. Remember, strong relationships are based on trust — and on genuine reciprocity, which can't be forced.

• **Find out contact preferences.** Show that you value the other person's time (and that you look forward to continuing the connection) by making sure you've exchanged contact information, and by finding out how he or she prefers to be contacted.

• **Follow the golden rule.** Above all, be considerate. If you behave in a way that is inconsiderate, you'll create a negative impression that outweighs whatever you are trying to offer. Always treat the other person as you would like to be treated.

After you get together. If your encounter sparked a positive connection, don't let the glow fade through lack of attention. Instead, strengthen it in the following ways:

- **Record contact information.** If you haven't done so already, enter the other person's contact information in your contact manager (or address book, or whatever other method you use for storing contact information). Make sure to note what you learned about how he or she prefers to be contacted; that way, you can begin your next interaction as positively as possible.

- **Note key details from your meeting.** While the meeting is still fresh in your mind, make a note of what you discussed and what you learned about the other person (interests, background, current projects, friends, and so on). Also, be sure to note any future plans the two of you made on your calendar. If your contact manager includes note-taking and calendar capabilities, you can connect all of this information with the person's contact details to recall it easily in the future.

- **Note the other person's network connections.** One of the most important aspects of creating Orbits is understanding how other people are connected to you and to others. Make a note of who you know in common, as well as of the other person's significant relationships. Remembering who works with this person may be important in the future, and his or her friendships may be important as well. Keep in mind the idea of "contagious happiness" we discussed in Chapter 2; "friends of friends" do affect us!

- **Respect the other person's privacy.** Use discretion with respect to sharing details from your meeting with anyone else. If you blog, tweet, or post about your get-together, you make your relationship less personal, and you lose a chance to build trust by protecting the other person's privacy. Also, be aware that corporate sleuthing firms do monitor social-media posts for competitive information, and even such seemingly innocent data as who's lunching with whom can be valuable intelligence; the headline of a recent news story on this topic, "Corporate spies mine for gold on social media," says it all.

- **Follow up in a meaningful way.** Keep the relationship moving forward by following up quickly — ideally within 24 hours — with a note of appreciation. Let the other person know you enjoyed getting together and appreciated the time he or she spent with you. Don't try to solicit a response; simply offer a respectful "tip of your hat" and leave the decision of whether to respond up to the other person.

- **Be patient.** Sometimes it can take time and repeated effort to establish a connection with someone. Of course, this effort should always be considerate. It's never a good idea to pester or stalk someone, which would produce the opposite result from what you are seeking. Instead, simply offer your friendship, be there for the other person, and allow time to determine if the seeds you've dropped have fallen on fertile ground. If the potential for friendship is there, these small gestures can develop over time into a deep and supportive relationship.

The approach outlined in these suggestions will help you to make the type of vital, personal connections that draw you into others' Orbits, and that invite them into yours. Once you've made those orbital connections, all you need to do is figure out how to maintain them (in a way that isn't too time-intensive), so they can enrich your existing social networks and leverage the potential of those networks. Fortunately, that process is the topic of our one remaining chapter.

 **CHAPTER SIX**

Maintaining Your Orbits

When you start making stronger, more orbital connections with others, you may feel a rush of euphoria — followed by a moment of panic, as you realize the level of intensity you've established in these relationships could be tough to maintain. After all, who's got that kind of time? Or that much mental bandwidth, in today's attention-deficit culture? Do you really have room in your life to go beyond Facebook-style friendships and connect with people on a deeper level?

Not to worry. While it's true that you need to invest some time in maintaining orbital relationships — as opposed to the zero-maintenance friendships you can have through social media — you can keep your time investment manageable. Plus, it's time well-spent, because you're creating social capital: a well of resources and support from which you and your fellow Orbit members can draw in times of need.

Also, while splitting your mental bandwidth among an increasing number of relationships can be challenging, keep in mind that technology can help. Your brain may not be hardwired to support significant relationships with more than 150 people (remember that Dunbar number in Chapter 4?), but some wisely chosen technological aid can help you use your mental bandwidth more productively.

The key to maintaining your Orbits in a non-time-intensive way is to develop some good relationship habits that make strategic use of supportive technology. The seven steps we'll discuss in this chapter are designed to build an effective Orbit-maintenance system through habits that develop their own momentum. Once you get them going, the effort becomes much less noticeable than the results.

Seven Steps to Sustaining Orbits

To maintain your Orbits, you need to sustain the relationships from which they're formed. That is, you need to stay in touch with the people in your Orbits in a meaningful way—giving them regular infusions of time, intensity, and consideration as you build trust and reciprocity.

The seven steps that follow will help you set up an efficient, easy-to-follow system for maintaining your Orbits:

1. Organize your Orbits

2. Track your interactions

3. Establish a weekly "stay in touch" time

4. Make your messages them-centric

5. Find creative ways to fit in face time

6. Sift your Orbits regularly

7. Complement depth with breadth

Before discussing these steps in detail, though, we need to say a few words about the technological capabilities we're going to recommend that you have. Because our company makes a contact manager that we ourselves use — and that we designed in accordance with our relationship philosophy—we naturally want to tell you how it can make the practices we're describing much easier. However, the last thing we want to do is seem like we are hyping our product. An emphasis on our own product would get in the way of our broader relationship message and undermine it, making this book seem us-centric instead of *you*-centric.

So, we decided to keep our technology recommendations general here and simply tell you what types of product features to look for. To find out more about our product, VIPorbit, and how it can help with the Orbit-maintenance steps discussed here, visit our company website at the following address: http://www.viporbit.com/

Step 1: Organize Your Orbits

All of your good intentions about maintaining strong relationships with the people in your Orbits will fall by the wayside if you can't remember who they all are, what you know about them, and how to reach them. You could, of course, keep lists of your Orbit members on paper and record contact information and notes in an address book or Rolodex. But those methods would be unwieldy and wouldn't offer instant retrieval of the information. The most time-saving method for organizing your Orbits is to use contact-management software — preferably with features that help you with your organizational tasks.

To help you keep your Orbits organized, your contact manager should provide features that let you perform the following tasks:

• Identify who's in your Orbits

• Define how Orbit members are connected to each other

• Store key information for each Orbit member

Let's take a closer look at each of these tasks and what capabilities it requires from your contact manager.

Identify Orbit members. To organize your Orbits easily within your contact manager, you'll need the ability to define groups. That way, you can define the Orbits to which each person belongs and display lists of the people in each Orbit. This capability is extremely helpful for remembering who's in each Orbit and for finding people quickly by context — for example, finding one of your friends in the media by opening up your "Media" Orbit.

If possible, use a contact manager that lets you put people in more than one group, since Orbits often overlap in real life. For example, you might have a cousin who's in the media and who shares your interest in mountain biking; you could put that person in your Family, Media, and Biking Orbits. Or, you might have a business relationship with someone who fits into multiple professional Orbits — as with technology evangelist and author Robert Scoble, who belongs to seven of Mike's Orbits: Media, Bloggers, Silicon Valley, Thought Leaders, Industry Acquaintances, Strategic, and VIPs.

We should note that, if you are a Google+ user, the Circles feature of Google+ gives you a way to represent your Orbits within Google+. However, we don't recommend using Google+ Circles as your primary Orbit organizer because it requires that your Orbit members also be Google+ members and because (as of this writing) it lacks capabilities that are important for Orbit maintenance, such as being able to store notes about each Orbit member, search easily for information about Orbit members, and maintain a comprehensive relationship history. Also, while Google+ appears to offer better privacy controls than Facebook does, it is still oriented toward public interactions, rather than the private interactions essential for maintaining strong relationships.

Define connections. Once you've identified who's in your Orbits, you can easily review who's connected to you, but what about their connections to each other? Just because you've identified two people as being in your Music Orbit, for example, doesn't mean they know each other. Knowing how people are connected to each other helps you understand what spheres of resource and influence they inhabit. It also helps you figure out how you can provide value to them by connecting them to each other.

Of course, you may be using a social-media product such as LinkedIn to keep track of how some of the people in your Orbits are connected to each other, but having this information in your contact manager lets you keep track of connections among all of your Orbit members, not just those who are your social media contacts — and it lets you do so privately.

Look for a contact manager that lets you easily create links between contacts and use this capability to note (and view) how your Orbit members are connected to each other.

Store key information. All contact managers store people's basic contact information, but if you want to sustain strong relationships, you'll also want user-definable fields for storing the types of information you consider important in connecting you with others. People's interests, hobbies, and fan relationships (such as the sports teams a person follows) are well worth setting up fields to store, as this information helps you reconnect on a personal level. You might also set up fields to store people's birthdays and the names of other important people in their lives (assistants, spouses, kids — and other Orbit members this person knows, if your contact manager doesn't have linking capabilities). You'll also want to create fields that relate to whatever professional connection you have with people; for example, if you deal with products or services for animals, you would probably want fields describing your Orbit members' pets (number of pets, types, names).

If your contact manager doesn't automatically track your interactions with people (more on that capability in a moment) and let you create To Do items for following up afterward, you'll definitely want one or more fields for recording notes after you interact with an Orbit member. For example, you'd want a field in which you could note "Ask how ski trip went" after an encounter like the one with the CEO "Mr. X" in Chapter 5.

If necessary, you could record all of the information mentioned here in a single "Notes" field, instead of in individual fields, but finding specific information within that field would be more difficult than finding it in a separate, searchable field.

Step 2: Track Your Interactions

The simple habit of logging your interactions with others in your contact manager can provide tremendous value in keeping your relationships strong. We're not talking about anything time-consuming — just a brief record of when each encounter occurred, what you discussed or learned, whether you made future plans, and what follow-up is needed. (See the "After you get together" section of Chapter 5 for more on this topic.)

Why do we recommend keeping this information in your contact manager, instead of simply in your calendar and To Do lists? Because, when it's in your contact manager, it constitutes a history of your relationship with each Orbit member. You can then retrieve that history when you're going to encounter someone again, to help you remember points of personal connection and easily resume the relationship. Have you ever described the experience of seeing an old friend as one of "picking up right where we last left off, as if no time had passed"? Well, an easy-to-access relationship history can help give you that kind of strong reconnection with everyone in your Orbits.

Another benefit of having a relationship history in your contact manager is that it provides an easy way to check which Orbit members you haven't been in touch with lately, reminding you to reconnect — as we'll discuss in Step 3.

To make the process of tracking your interactions as easy as possible, look for a contact manager that runs on your smartphone and is integrated with your calendar, To Do list, and all of your modes of communication (for example, Skype, SMS, email, Facebook, and Twitter). If it runs on your smartphone, you'll have it handy wherever you go, so you can take notes right after you get together with people (as well as retrieve relationship histories on the fly, when you encounter Orbit members unexpectedly). And, if your contact manager is integrated with your calendar and To Do list, it can automatically store a record of completed activities related to each Orbit member. Finally, integration of your contact manager with email and other communication modes can provide automatic tracking of your communications with each Orbit member — all you need to do is initiate communication from within the contact manager.

Step 3: Establish a Weekly "Stay in Touch" Time

Once you have an easy-to-peruse list of Orbit members, with information about each relationship at your fingertips, how do you keep those relationships going? Some of your Orbit members are people you often see or talk to in the course of your daily activities, but what about the rest? It's easy to let those relationships weaken, thinking, "Well, I just don't have the time to connect with everyone," or, "They're probably reading my status updates, so we're basically connected."

Actually, they're probably as busy as you are, which means they aren't necessarily keeping up with any or all messages you broadcast publicly. And if they *are* reading your status updates, that experience won't be personal enough to strengthen your connection; it will lack the elements of attentive time, emotional intensity, and trust-building privacy (as well as reciprocity, if they don't comment on your updates).

Fortunately, the groundwork you've laid in organizing your Orbits and updating your relationship histories pays off in a big way when it comes to making sure you stay in touch with people. You can easily scroll through a list of your Orbit members, see who you haven't been in touch with as recently as you'd like, and send those folks a quick "hello" message. Or, if you know they prefer phone to email, call them; even if you just leave voicemail messages, you've made them aware that you're thinking of them. Think of this as a small but important relationship-maintenance signal, reminding them that you care.

We recommend that you set aside a regular time to send out these signals each week — say, Friday at 12:30 (or whatever time works best for you, of course). We also recommend that you create an Orbit or group called something like "Touch Base," so that you can put people in it whenever you think, "I've got to remember to touch base with so-and-so, but I don't have time right now." If you do so, your weekly stay-in-touch time becomes even easier, since you have a ready-made list of people to contact during that time. Once you've contacted them, you can move them out of that Orbit until the next time you realize it's time to get in touch with them again.

Not sure what to say in your stay-in-touch messages? We'll talk about that next.

Step 4: Make Your Messages Them-Centric

When you're dashing off a stay-in-touch message to someone in your Orbit, put yourself in the other person's head for a moment. Think about what kind of message from you would be welcome.

If the recipient is a person you've been intending to contact for a particular reason, you'll already have a message in mind. In that case, just write the message, then review it quickly to check that you've been considerate of the recipient's time and feelings. If you were receiving this message, would it give you a positive impression of the sender's regard for you? If not, reword it in a more considerate way.

If the message is simply meant to keep the relationship going, what to say may not be as obvious. Here's what you need to know: The purpose of a stay-in-touch message is to give the recipient a moment of your one-on-one attention — without asking for anything in return. So, say something that appreciates the other person or provides value to him or her, with no pressure for a response. If you need ideas, take a moment to review your relationship history or what you've noted about the other person's interests to put you in the frame of mind to make a personal connection. Give the recipient of your message a chance to enjoy your attention for a moment, creating a positive feeling that nourishes the connection between the two of you.

Here are some ideas for types of stay-in-touch messages that appreciate or provide value to others without creating any pressure to respond:

• **Reminded-of-you-by messages.** "I just saw [*so-and-so / such-and-such*], and was reminded of when you and I got together to [*do whatever we did*]. We should do that again sometime—I enjoyed it. Let me know next time you're available and interested in [*repeating the experience*]."

- **Thank-you messages.** "Just wanted to thank you again for the [*time you spent with me / suggestion you gave me / hospitality you showed me*] when we got together at [*time and place x*]. It really helped me with [*such-and such*]. Let me know if I can return the favor sometime."

- **Opportunity messages.** "Just heard about an [*event / job opening / available apartment / other opportunity*] that made me think of [*you / your situation*], so I thought I'd pass along the info, in case it's useful to you…"

- **Competitive-awareness messages.** "I happened to find out that [*company or person x in your industry is planning to take strategic action y*] and thought you might like to know…"

- **Congratulations messages.** "Just heard the news about your [*promotion / engagement / baby / book / other achievement*] and wanted to extend my congratulations."

Notice that all of these messages are them-centric — focusing on them, the recipients, rather than on you — and personal in their appreciation. The relationship history and notes in your Orbit information will help you find something specific to say to each person. You can also consult people's publicly posted social-media information for news or details about them.

Step 5: Find Creative Ways to Fit in Face Time

While regular messages are important signals of your attention to a relationship, they don't provide the intensity or two-way interaction of "face time" — time you spend interacting with each other, able to read and respond to each other's facial cues. Ideally, this is time you spend in each other's physical presence, where body language provides an additional level of communication, but you can also count face-to-face technology such as videoconferencing as a form of face time.

Fitting in face time with others is, of course, more challenging than finding time to send brief messages. It takes more time — both yours and theirs — and requires planning and logistical considerations. But if you think creatively, you can find ways to fit more face time into activities you'd be doing anyway, so the effort is minimal.

Once a week, try finding a person in your Orbits to connect with you in one of the following ways (or in another way that you come up with):

• Get together for a meal

• Meet for a coffee or tea break

• Exercise together — take a walk, ride bikes, play a game of golf or tennis

• Walk your dogs together

• Carpool together to an event you're both attending

• Talk face-to-face via a videoconferencing app (such as Skype or FaceTime)

Fitting in face time with one person once a week may not sound like enough effort to maintain a significant Orbit, but remember: moments matter. Your 50 or so face-to-face encounters during the year may well be the equivalent of Hillary Clinton's visits to 50 countries in a year: the incremental investments of time that build trust and emotional connections.

Speaking of globe-trotting: Keep in mind that travel is a great opportunity for meeting up with far-flung Orbit members face-to-face and in person. When you're making travel plans, think about who you know in your destination city (or do a search in your contact manager) — then let them know you'll be in town and would value a chance to get together. And if you live in a city that's a travel destination for others, offer to introduce them to a favorite restaurant or a non-time-intensive local attraction when they're in town.

Step 6: Sift Your Orbits Regularly

"OK," you may be saying, "I guess I can arrange for face time with one person each week and send out 'stay in touch' messages once a week, but what if my Orbits get so big that they need more time than I can devote to them?"

Then it's time to sift — as in, sift some people *out* of your Orbits.

It may seem strange that we're going to talk about removing people from your Orbits after we've devoted a substantial amount of this book to discussing how to develop your Orbits. However, Orbits fulfill their purpose only if they're composed of strong relationships. If a relationship fails to thrive despite the attention you give it (limited though that may be), that attention would be better spent elsewhere.

Sifting doesn't mean shunning people or deleting them from your contact manager (though you can, of course, take either action in drastic circumstances). It simply means no longer expending effort to stay in touch or otherwise maintain the relationship. We recommend that you create an Orbit or group called "Out of Orbit" and move people's information into it when you decide to sift them out of your regular Orbits. Then, you can easily ignore them when you're sending "stay in touch" messages and arranging face time — but you can still access their contact information if you need to reach them for some reason, or if you decide to reactivate your relationship later on.

Who should you sift out of your Orbits? Let's think back to the elements of a strong relationship: time, intensity, trust, reciprocity, and consideration.

Basically, you might want to sift people out when your relationships with them fail to thrive due to one or more of the following critical weaknesses:

- **Inattentiveness:** They never seem to have time for you.

- **Lack of intensity:** There's no emotional connection between you.

- **Lack of trust:** They behave in an unreliable or untrustworthy manner, their values and yours seem far apart, or they seem unable or unwilling to trust you.

- **One-way effort:** They don't reciprocate your efforts to develop the relationship.

- **Lack of consideration:** They show a pattern of treating you in an inconsiderate manner.

As for when to sift your Orbits, you can set a regular time to do it, such as once a month, or do it whenever your Orbits start to feel unmanageable. If you keep your Orbit information on your smartphone or other portable device, you can easily fit in Orbit sifting when you're in a mobile situation with time on your hands, such as waiting at an airport. Just scroll through the names of your Orbit members, and when you encounter a relationship that's nonessential and critically weak, move that person to "Out of Orbit." If the relationship revives at a later date, you can move the person back to one of your regular Orbits.

Step 7: Complement Depth with Breadth

You're well on the path now to maintaining Orbits of deeper, stronger relationships. But before we wrap up, we'd like to circle back for a moment to a concept we discussed in the first chapter: the idea of bringing relationships into balance. That is, balancing the breadth and outreach of social media with the depth-oriented culture of Orbits. As you move deeper into the realm of Orbital relationships, how do you fit these relationships into the larger social-media landscape?

Actually, your social-media realm can complement your Orbits, if you make strategic use of what it offers: a way to reach out to others widely and broadly in a public way.

We suggest using social media to perform the following tasks, which use breadth to complement the depth of your orbital relationships:

- **Find and contact people** with whom you'd like to initiate or reestablish a relationship, exploring outside your immediate friendship circles to locate others who share your passions and spark your ideas (you can then follow up with orbital strategies to deepen the connection)

- **Read people's public information** (profiles, status updates, blogs, tweets, and so on) when you want to learn more about the personalities, backgrounds, relationships, and interests of those with whom you'd like to create a stronger personal connection (as described in Chapter 5)

- **Publicize information of your own** that you want to be widely known (while sharing more-strategic information privately to build trust with selected people)

- **Mobilize others for group actions** in situations where you feel such action is called for — finding out who responds will connect you more deeply with others who share your passions

- **Participate in or create virtual communities** of people with shared interests or goals (for example, Facebook groups of people working on a project together, or developer-and-customer groups like Apple AppStore community) — not only do such groups aid collaboration and accelerate innovation, they can also initiate connections for you to develop into strong Orbits

- **Solicit public feedback** about products or ideas, so you can improve them (thus strengthening your relationship with customers or fans by showing consideration and reciprocity)

While the number of significant relationships you have with others may be hard-wired into your brain, as Robin Dunbar's research suggests, you can use social media to cast a wider net to find that core group of people, seeking those whose interests, actions, and ideas complement and inspire yours. Instead of maxing out your Orbits with the people who happen to live near you, you can create Orbits of like-minded people from all over the world.

Starting Your Orbital Journey

Social networking technology has empowered us all with the ability to reach out to each other in previously unimagined ways: effortlessly, across wide distances and social or business hierarchies, and with lightning speed. By increasing the flow of ideas across a wider range of people, this technology has sped revolutionary changes across societies and business communities. However, the pace of this change has led many of us to leap on board so quickly that we haven't noticed what we're leaving behind: meaningful, two-way connections. We've amassed a vast network of social-media "friendships," but we have few real friends — and not as many truly successful business relationships as we would like.

When you look up from this book, we hope you'll see your social networks in a new way: no longer as a random crisscross of mostly meaningless connections, but as a wealth of potentially priceless relationships. By nurturing those connections with a little time and attention, generating a spark of emotional intensity, and applying the steady warmth of trust-building consideration, you can invite them to grow from weak links into strong, two-way bonds — bonds that pull you into each others' powerful and sustaining Orbits.

We hope the insights and strategies we've provided here will provide a detailed-enough road map — or galaxy map? — to answer the questions that come up as you begin your orbital journey. If not, though talk to us. Make this a two-way conversation by sending us your questions and your feedback at www.whosinyourorbit.com. We look forward to connecting with you.

But first, it's time for you to tackle that question you've been waiting to answer:

Who's in your Orbit?

NOTES

Chapter One: Who Are All These "Friends," Anyway?

The experiment of posting multiple Facebook birthdays in a single month (and getting multiple birthday greetings from oblivious well-wishers) is described in the following online article: "My Fake Facebook Birthdays: What happened when I celebrated my Facebook birthday on July 11. And July 25. And July 28." By David Plotz, *Slate* magazine, August 2, 2011: http://www.slate.com/id/2300637/pagenum/all/ - p2

The glowing review of the Facebook Timeline feature—in which reviewer Sam Biddle described the Timeline-enhanced Facebook as feeling like "a monument to yourself" and "your best new altar"—was posted on September 23, 2011, under the title "Facebook Timeline Review: This Is the Greatest Thing Facebook's Ever Done," on the website gizmodo.com: http://gizmodo.com/5843354/facebook-timeline-review-this-is-the-greatest-thing-facebooks-ever-done

To learn more about the pioneering work of the German sociologist Georg Simmel in the early 1900s, which paved the way for the study of social networking, consult the chapter on Simmel in *Sociological Theory*, 6th Edition, by George Ritzer and Douglas J. Goodman (New York: McGraw-Hill, 2004), beginning on page 153.

To read Max's thoughts on the benefits of social networking technology as a driving force for innovation, consult his blog, "Welcome to the Real (IT) World!" (Of particular note is the entry titled "The Complexity of Simplicity," dated July 6, 2011.) You can find Max's blog online at: http://isismjpucher.wordpress.com/

Chapter Two: Why Strong Relationships Matter

Winston Churchill's comment about Hitler invading Hell is quoted by Andrew Nagorski in *The Greatest Battle* (Simon & Schuster, 2007), pages 150-151.

For details of James Fowler's and Nicholas Christakis' study on "contagious happiness," see "Dynamic spread of happiness in a large social network: longitudinal analysis over 20 years in the Framingham Heart Study," *BMJ* (British Medical Journal) 337 (2008): a2338.

Chapter Three: What Makes Relationships Strong—and Orbital

Our formulation of the components of relationship strength comes originally from an article by sociologist Mark Granovetter: "The Strength of Weak Ties," *American Journal of Sociology* 78 (1973): 1360-1380. However, we used a slightly different version of the component names, following the lead of social media scientist Michael Wu in his article "Figuring Out the Relationship Puzzle," on the Lithium lithosphere website: http://lithosphere.lithium.com/t5/Building-Community-the-Platform/Figuring-Out-the-Relationship-Puzzle/ba-p/11290.

Chapter Four: What's Grounding Your Orbits

The study about stressful Facebook use was described in the following newspaper article: "Facebook 'friends' cause stress, anxiety," *Silicon Valley/San Jose Business Journal*, February 21, 2011.

Thomas H. Davenport's characterization of attention as being today's most important scarce resource comes from the following article: "eLearning and the Attention Economy: Here, There, and Everywhere?" *LiNE Zine*, Summer 2001, available at http://linezine.com/5.2/articles/tdeatae.htm.

For the full story behind the Dunbar Number, see Robin Dunbar's book *Grooming, Gossip, and the Evolution of Language* (Harvard University Press, 1998). Or, check out the discussion of the Dunbar Number in Malcolm Gladwell's *The Tipping Point – How Little Things Make a Big Difference* (Little, Brown and Company, 2000), 177–181 and 185–186.

For an argument that 291 is a more typical network size than 148 (the Dunbar Number) at the start of the 21st century, see the following article: C. McCarty, P.D. Killworth, H.R. Bernard, E. Johnsen, and G. Shelley, "Comparing Two Methods for Estimating Network Size," *Human Organization* 60, No. 1 (2001) 28–39.

Robin Dunbar's account of finding confirmation of the Dunbar Number in virtual worlds, along with his explanation of the type of relationships this number is meant to represent, can be found in his article "The Magic Number" in the Spring 2010 *RSA Journal*: http://www.thersa.org/fellowship/journal/archive/spring-2010/features/the-magic-number

Lauren Silverman's August 2008 radio commentary "Public is the New Private" can be found on the NPR (National Public Radio) website at: http://www.npr.org/templates/story/story.

php?storyId=93374338

For coverage of Facebook's loosening of user privacy boundaries (and video of founder Mark Zuckerberg discussing this shift), see Marshall Kirkpatrick's article "Facebook's Zuckerberg Says the Age of Privacy is Over" on the ReadWriteWeb website: http://www.readwriteweb.com/archives/facebooks_zuckerberg_says_the_age_of_privacy_is_ov.php

Chapter Five: Connecting Strongly With Others

"Inside the State Department," the National Geographic documentary chronicling a year in the professional life of Secretary of State Hillary Clinton aired on November 8, 2010.

Abstract on Mike Muhney:

Born and raised in Chicago, Mike is a graduate of the University of Illinois, College of Commerce. Mike began his career with IBM in the pre-PC era and was trained as a Marketing Representative and enjoyed a very successful sales career with IBM until the entrepreneurial bug bit him.

In 1986 Mike and a friend co-founded the company Contact Software International and they co-invented ACT!™ which is credited with creating the category of Contact Management applications. ACT!™ also has been frequently credited with pioneering today's CRM (Customer Relationship Management) industry. Released in 1987, ACT!™ went on to win over 100 awards globally, including numerous PC Magazine Editor's Choice awards (the "Oscar" of any and all PC Industry Awards), and is still, after these many years, the predominant desktop Contact Manager. Mike and his partner sold their company in 1993 to Symantec and realized very handsome returns for all stakeholders in the organization.

Mike believes that there is infinite value in closer relationships whatever their slant and that this not only includes salespeople but everyone else as well seeing that no matter what we do, we all deal with people and can improve and expand our base of social and business relationships. As a passionate technology visionary, Mike has devoted his career to focusing on the power of sustainable relationships, and the vital importance of the human element, and combining that with software solutions that affect that.

Frequently sought after as an inspiring speaker and expert on relationship management, Mike is again taking his passion for public speaking, his commitment to education, and his wealth of experience in global sales, marketing, and entrepreneurship to those looking to excel in their own interpersonal relationships and gain a competitive edge. For more information on Mike's schedule and availability, send inquiries to Mike@viporbit.com.

ACT!™ is a registered TM of Sage PLC.

Abstract on Max J. Pucher:

Max was born in 1954 in Austria, where he grew up in the gas lit streets of postwar suburb Vienna. After college he joined IBM as an engineer, first servicing cardpunch devices. In international assignments in the UK and Saudi Arabia he became an expert in IBM mainframe technology. In the final years of his 15-year IBM career, Max worked in Austria in software consulting and finally in sales.

In 1988 Max left IBM to found ISIS Papyrus Software, today a medium-size, worldwide operating software company for content and process management solutions for 2000 large enterprises. Max believes that technology betters our lives if it is made for people and with people in mind. He invented and designed the concept for the Papyrus Platform, which is the first technology that enables the embedded use of machine-learning, 'artificial intelligence' functionality that learns to perform business activity from human interaction in real-time. In 2005 he stepped down as the CEO to focus on his role as Chief Architect and on further expanding the platform for mobile applications and for people empowerment. Max holds several patents, and frequently writes and speaks on information, people and business management subjects.

Max has written several fiction and non-fiction books and is honored to collaborate with Mike Muhney on 'Who's in Your Orbit?' Max and Mike are living proof of how technology shapes our relationships and lives as they did meet through a social network despite being nearly neighbors in Texas. For Max, the message of this book is that software and technology is not about cost-cutting efficiency, but more importantly about people empowerment and quality of life. Relationships are not improved by a database of acquaintances, but by better communication. Max wants to show you how the use of state-of-the-art technology can make a huge difference in your relationships. For more information on Max's schedule and availability, send inquiries to Max@viporbit.com.

Who's In YOUR Orbit?